In
CLASSICAL
mood

Party Time

Party Time

*A*ny joyous occasion can be marked by a party—
from a special family celebration to grand events
on a national scale. Knowing this, many composers have
written splendid music for all kinds of festivities. From the
intoxicating rush of Mozart's aria for the hero of *Don
Giovanni* to the cultured sparkle of Chopin's *Waltz in E-flat
Major*, each piece in this volume of In Classical Mood
conjures up its own individual party atmosphere. Dvořák's
Carnival Overture and Chabrier's "Fête polonaise" are on
a grand scale while Respighi's "Badinage" captures the
intimate atmosphere of friends gossiping in a corner.
Whatever your celebration, let *Party Time* set the mood.

THE LISTENER'S GUIDE — WHAT THE SYMBOLS MEAN

THE COMPOSERS
Their lives... their loves...
their legacies...

THE MUSIC
Explanation... analysis...
interpretation...

THE INSPIRATION
How works of genius
came to be written

THE BACKGROUND
People, places, and events
linked to the music

© MCMXCVIII IMP AB   In Classical Mood™   IMP AB, produced under license by IMP Inc.   Printed in China.   US P 2201 12 036

Contents

HANS CHRISTIAN LUMBYE *1810–1874*

Champagne Galop

OPUS 14

Perfect for getting the party going, this infectious piece was written for the 1845 Tivoli Gardens music festival in Copenhagen, where Lumbye served as musical director for 29 years. Fanfare and the distinctive pop of a champagne cork spark off the festivities, and from this point on, the frantic tempo of the Galop scarcely pauses. A simple, jolly tune highlighted by the piccolo is perfectly offset by the bouncing rhythm. A central section on the xylophone is deliberately gentle, so that the toe-tapping can return with renewed vigor and the music build to its finale. The piece ends suitably with a final pop—a promise of more fun to come.

THE FROTH OF FUN

No celebration is complete without champagne—the most famous sparkling wine in the world. According to tradition, this exhilarating "bubbly" was created by a monk. Dom Pierre Pérignon (1638–1715), cellar-master at the Abbey of Hautevilliers in Champagne, north-eastern France, came up with the idea of allowing the local white wine, "vin gris," to ferment in the bottle by adding yeast, making it fizzy. "I am seeing stars!" was the delighted Dom's verdict (*left*). It is this second fermentation in the bottle (the first takes place, as with any other wine, in the vat) that defines the "méthode champenoise," the zealously guarded qualification of champagne, which can only refer to wines from Champagne vineyards (*right*). Since Dom Pérignon's happy discovery, the wine's reputation continued to grow unabated, making the towns of Reims and Épernay world-famous for

such brands as Mumm, Roederer, Krug, Moët-Chandon and Veuve Clicquot-Ponsardin—the firm of the Widow Clicquot (*left*). Symbol of wealth, power and fun, champagne reached its fashionable height at the end of the 19th century, when it seemed that much of the prosperous world was at one long party. International sales peaked again during the 1980s, reflecting the conspicuous consumption of the "yuppie" years. But fittingly, it is in its homeland, France, that this drink of joy and celebration has to satisfy the greatest demand.

CAVORTING COUPLES

The galop became one of the most popular dances of the 19th century. Originating in Germany, it took off in Vienna in the 1820s, before spreading to France and England. The name of the dance comes from the wild galloping steps with which couples leap around the ballroom. Most galops are short as few can keep up the frantic pace for long. The dance's brief, rollicking nature provided a stirring finale to many a ball, and from the ballroom it found its way into ballet, and then light opera. Among the composers who wrote for this lively form were Schubert, Johann Strauss II and Liszt. The galop survived well into the 20th century, with the Russian composers Prokofiev, Khachaturian and Shostakovich using it in their scores.

The breathless pace of the galop usually resulted in collision on the dancefloor.

OPEN-AIR ENTERTAINMENT

Pleasure gardens, such as the Tivoli of Copenhagen, were also popular in 18th-century London. The most famous and long-lasting were those of Vauxhall (*left*). For a small entrance fee visitors could enjoy various diversions which culminated in an evening concert, with songs, overtures, symphonies and opera.

KEY NOTES

As well as this light music for the Tivoli Gardens, Lumbye composed other types of dance music for the theater, and dances for the ballet at the Royal Theatre in Copenhagen, including three other galops.

FRÉDÉRIC CHOPIN *1810–1849*

Waltz in E-flat Major

OPUS 18

GRANDE VALSE BRILLANTE

Chopin wrote this piece shortly after arriving in Vienna in 1830, where the public was in the grip of the waltz craze, which the 21-year-old composer obviously joined in. However, in his "Grand Brilliant Waltz," Chopin produced a unique and exquisitely balanced piece, in complete contrast to the brash Viennese style. This piece is full of the grace and fluidity so typical of Chopin's music.

VERSATILE WORK

Chopin wrote this waltz in Vienna but it was in Paris, where he moved in 1831, that it shot to fame. It was named "Grande valse brillante" when it was published there in 1834.

KEY NOTES

Although Chopin did not write his waltzes for dancers, Mikhail Fokine included this one in the 1909 production of his ballet Les Sylphides.

EMMANUEL CHABRIER *1841–1894*

Le Roi malgré lui

FÊTE POLONAISE

This richly orchestrated piece accompanies one of the most magnificent ballroom scenes in opera. Opening Act Two, it serves as an overture, while also conveying all the splendor of a lavish ball. "The Reluctant King" has come to a court ball in disguise, after hearing of a plot to overthrow him. The preliminaries to these "Polish Festivities" are deceptively formal, but that only serves to highlight the frolic in store, for a loud drum beat announces more exuberant music. An outburst reaches a heart-stopping climax and then gives way to lilting dance music. Finally, like fireworks in the night sky, the riotous earlier theme bursts through again, bringing the magnificent revelries to a rousing end.

AN INTERRUPTED RUN

A fire in Paris's Opéra-Comique cut short the first run of this opera in 1887, after three nights. The show resumed after the building was restored.

THE RELUCTANT KING

Le Roi malgré lui is set in the 16th century, when a French prince, Henry of Valois (*left*), succeeded to the throne of Poland. He and his nobles discover a plot led by the Polish Count Laski to replace him with the Archduke of Austria. Henry, however, secretly wants the plot to succeed so that he may return to France. At a masked ball attended by the conspirators, he presents his friend Nangis to them disguised as king. They now reveal to Henry that they intend to kill the monarch. Nangis manages to escape, and Henry also tries to flee the country. However, before the king can leave Poland, he meets a troop of French soldiers who tell him that the conspiracy has failed. Henry must return—reluctantly—to continue his reign.

REBUILDING PARIS

In the 19th century, Paris changed beyond recognition. On the orders of Emperor Napoleon III, Baron Haussmann (*right*, shown as an industrious beaver) gave the French capital a radical facelift. The diligent builder embarked on a 27-year re-planning of the city, demolishing the jumble of narrow, medieval streets and replacing them with wide open squares (*left*), and the famous grand boulevards.

KEY NOTES

Chabrier's teacher, the Polish violinist Tarnowski, may have inspired this operetta's theme and music. Under his influence, Chabrier had already written several Czech- and Polish-style dances.

GIUSEPPE VERDI *1813–1901*

La Traviata

BRINDISI

In this famous scene from Verdi's opera, the hero Alfredo leads party guests in a drinking song or *Brindisi*. The heroine Violetta, who is attracted to Alfredo, takes up the second stanza, and the duo ends up singing the rousing theme together, with support from the rest of the company: "Drink, drink from the goblets of joy." The atmosphere of merriment and the carefree music provide a painful contrast to the tragic tale that unfolds. Directly after this happy moment, Violetta is overcome by a coughing fit, a symptom of tuberculosis, the disease that she has kept secret and which will eventually kill her.

A WOMAN WRONGED

The moving story of *La Traviata* is famous for melting the hardest of hearts. The title translates as "The Fallen Woman," and refers to Violetta, a 19th-century Parisian courtesan with a string of rich, upper-class lovers. However, when she falls in love with Alfredo, she decides to reform and settles down with him, living a quiet life in the country just outside Paris. But soon afterward, Alfredo's father calls on Violetta and persuades her to leave his son: his daughter's fiancé refuses to accept the liaison between Violetta and Alfredo and is threatening to break off his engagement as a matter of honor. She yields to his arguments and flees, leaving Alfredo to presume that she has left him for another man. The wounded Alfredo publicly insults her, then is told the truth of her sacrifice by his father (*left*). He rushes back to her, but she is now gravely ill, and he arrives only just in time to declare his love for her before she dies.

FIRST PRODUCTION

The subject of *La Traviata* was deemed too shocking in Italy for performance without censorship. As a result, an 18th-century setting (*above*) was dictated by the contract for the premiere, even though Verdi insisted that a contemporary setting was crucial for emotional impact. His librettist, Piave, felt that the quality of the opera company was inferior, but did not tell Verdi. These misgivings were confirmed at the first night in Venice in 1853. Verdi wrote to a friend, "I am sorry to have to give you the sad news. *La Traviata* was a fiasco." The performace must have been awful— *La Traviata* is now recognized as one of Verdi's masterpieces.

DUMAS THE YOUNGER

La Dame aux camélias, the play on which Verdi based *La Traviata*, was written by Alexandre Dumas the younger (*right*). He was the illegitimate son of the French novelist and playwright, also called Alexandre, who was the author of *The Count of Monte Cristo* and *The Three Musketeers*. With *La Dame aux camélias*, produced in 1852 and adapted from an earlier novel, the younger Dumas shot to fame. It was inspired by a beautiful Parisian courtesan, Marie Duplessis (*left*), whom Dumas had loved. Exactly the same age as she was, he was greatly affected by her death at the age of 23. Social observation and criticism became the central topics of all Dumas's ensuing works. Before dying at age 71, he was elected to the Académie Française, and established himself as France's foremost playwright.

AN ANCIENT PROFESSION

The word courtesan comes from "cortigiana", an old Italian word for a female courtier. For centuries cultivated women, such as Madame de Pompadour, mistress of Louis XV (*right*), wielded great influence at royal courts. After the monarchy was toppled in France, courtesans turned their attentions to rich and influential men in society. Dumas based *La Dame aux camélias* on this new generation of courtesans.

KEY NOTES

Despite Verdi's objections, Fanny Salvini-Donatelli, a rather plump soprano, was chosen as the first Violetta. Unfortunately, the audience began to laugh as she tried to portray the fragile Violetta.

CHARLES GOUNOD *1818–1893*

Faust

BALLET MUSIC NO.1

A brief but imposing introduction with discordant harmonies sets an ominous mood before the music melts into a more light-hearted theme. This delightful waltz is one of the spectacles that Faust, who has sold his soul to the Devil in return for renewed youth, enjoys at the wicked Walpurgis Night celebrations. Traditionally believed to be held on the eve of May 1 in the Harz Mountains of central Germany, the festival involved a gathering of magical creatures. In this section from the ballet, famous figures from legend and history dance for the demonic audience.

OPERA MEETS BALLET

Gounod wrote this whimsical ballet for a production of *Faust* for the Paris Opéra in 1869, ten years after the opera's premiere.

KEY NOTES

By the time of Gounod's death, his opera Faust had, astonishingly, received more than a thousand performances.

JOSEPH HAYDN *1732–1809*

Trumpet Concerto in E-flat Major

THIRD MOVEMENT

Haydn wrote this concerto for the Viennese court trumpeter, Anton Weidinger, inventor of the keyed trumpet. This new trumpet could not only play more notes than its predecessor (the long, flared tube trumpet), it could also be played in more musical keys. Here Haydn explores these new possibilities with a passion. After a magnificent opening on strings, the trumpet comes in. At first it stays with the simple main melody, but soon it tackles more sophisticated phrases. While observing the refined tastes of the court, Haydn also manages to convey a sense of cheerful merrymaking.

A NEW INVENTION

In Haydn's early years, the trumpet was still the long, flared tube of former centuries (*left*), offering a very limited range and requiring great skill from the player. It was used mostly when a piece was in the key of D Major or kept in the background. Trumpeters could use shanks (extra tubing) to change the key. But this was cumbersome, and composers had to allow enough time in the music for the changeover. The keyed trumpet greatly improved matters. Its tone, however, was disappointing and it fell out of favor.

Today's modern valve trumpet can cater to both classical and jazz music, as demonstrated by the versatile Wynton Marsalis (*right*).

COURT COMPOSER

Haydn worked for 29 years at the Esterházy court in Hungary as musical director for Prince Nicholas (*left*). When Nicholas died in 1790, his son, Prince Anton, disbanded the court orchestra, and Haydn left to travel around Europe. Prince Anton died four years later, and the composer was recalled by the next prince. Soon after returning, Haydn wrote his famous *Trumpet Concerto*. He remained at the court until 1804, during which time he also wrote the "Emperor's Hymn" to boost the morale of Austria, which was at war with Napoleon. It is now the Austrian national anthem.

KEY NOTES

Surprisingly, Haydn's Trumpet Concerto *vanished from the concert repertoire soon after his death. It returned only as recently as 1928, when George Eskdale, the famous English trumpeter, made a broadcast of the piece and a classic recording on 78-r.p.m. record.*

WOLFGANG AMADEUS MOZART *1756–1791*

Don Giovanni

K527, "FINCH" HAN DAL VINO

*I*n this thrilling aria, performed at breakneck speed, Don Giovanni sings of his plans for a party even though he is being pursued by various characters, all of whom he has outraged. He is concerned only with finding more women to add to his list of conquests. The party is really a ploy to assemble as many potential lovers as possible, so that he can seduce them—"as soon as they have drunk the wine" ("Finch" han dal vino")! Mozart's jaunty music brilliantly evokes the freethinker's excitement as he envisages the joys of the revels to come.

PLEASURE BEFORE WORK

The evening before the premiere of *Don Giovanni* in Prague in 1787, Mozart went to a party, then worked all night on the music. He finished it at seven o'clock the next morning!

KEY NOTES

While writing **Don Giovanni,** *Mozart received a pupil whose skill at the piano greatly impressed him. The 16-year-old boy was none other than Ludwig van Beethoven.*

OTTORINO RESPIGHI *1879–1936*

Suite for Strings and Flute

BADINAGE

The word "badinage" means banter, and Respighi's music immediately evokes a gossipy gathering of friends. The violin, viola and cello imitate different voices in the group, with the flute piping up excitedly above them all. A new theme interrupts the happy chatter, representing a more serious topic of conversation, perhaps news of a love affair. But this seriousness is soon passed over and the flow of talk begins again before we can almost hear the friends bidding farewell to each other as the music draws to its close.

REVIVING A TRADITION

Instrumental music in Italy was replaced by opera after the Baroque period of Vivaldi and Corelli. It was Respighi, Ferruccio Busoni (1866–1924) and Ildebrando Pizzetti (1880–1968), who revived the instrumental tradition of Italy.

KEY NOTES

Respighi's skill as an orchestrator is linked to his Russian travels. From 1901 to 1903, he studied there with one of the greatest orchestrators ever, Rimsky-Korsakov.

JACQUES OFFENBACH *1819–1880*

La Grande-Duchesse de Gérolstein

OVERTURE

*J*acques Offenbach's *Overture* previews the main themes of his operetta. The piece mirrors the way in which love is rudely interrupted by war-mongering—as the story will soon reveal. With violins and trumpets and a hint of booming cannon, the first section introduces the royal setting of the story, full of pomp and ceremony.

A quieter string passage continues the royal idiom, but suggests a more private world. This leads into a tender love theme, with solo flute soaring above the strings and introducing a gentle interlude. This light, flowing theme is curtailed by a fanfare announcing a new melody: a bright, tripping tune that seems to be poking fun at the pompous military, as it makes its merry way to the end.

RIVAL SUCCESS

Offenbach took advantage of the World Exhibition of 1867 to gain popularity for *La Grande-Duchesse de Gérolstein*. However, his music was faced with a serious rival: Johann Strauss II's "Blue Danube" waltz was all the rage in Paris and threatened to overshadow Offenbach's success.

THE DUCHESS AND THE SOLDIER

The operetta satirizes the militarism of mid-19th-century Europe. The Grand Duchess (*left*) of a fictional country falls for a private soldier, Fritz. But the ambitious Fritz loves a peasant girl. When he relates his military strategy to the Grand Duchess, she is so impressed that she promotes him to general. He heads off to battle and duly wins a brilliant victory. The displaced General Boum is not happy with any of this, and plots to topple the new hero. The Grand Duchess, angry because Fritz has married his true love after all, joins in with this scheme. All ends with Fritz being reduced once more to the rank of private.

Hortense Schneider, the formidable first Grand Duchess of the title.

THE WORLD ON VIEW

The 1867 World Exhibition was the crowning event of the Second Empire of France. Napoleon III (1808–1873),

Napoleon Bonaparte's nephew, wanted it to attract international support for France, which was then increasingly in conflict with Prussia. Nations from around the world exhibited their products and exports (*left*, the Russian pavillion), and royalty from East and West converged on Paris to enjoy the exhibition—and the pleasures of "gay Paree."

KEY NOTES

When Hortense Schneider arrived at the World Exhibition in a carriage, a privilege reserved only for royalty, she gained access by declaring: "I am the Grand Duchess of Gérolstein!"

JOHANN STRAUSS II *1825–1899*

Die Fledermaus

OVERTURE

This famous *Overture* gives a foretaste of the sumptuous feast of music that lies ahead, including the "Fledermaus Waltz," with its delirious rhythm and seductive melody. The highlight of the *Overture*, and of the operetta, the waltz is the culmination of the ball in Act Two. In this lavish setting, Dr. Falke exacts a light-hearted revenge on his friend Gabriel Eisenstein. Falke has acquired the nickname "Die Fledermaus" (the bat), thanks to an earlier prank by Eisenstein that left the doctor dressed as a bat in public. He persuades Eisenstein and his wife to attend a masked ball— separately. The plan works: Eisenstein flirts with a lovely Hungarian lady who, in the end, turns out to be his wife!

THE WALTZ KING

Johann Strauss II was born in 1825, the eldest son of the great Viennese waltz composer, also Johann, whose name he made even more famous. At six years old, Johann II composed his first bars of waltz music which his mother wrote down and titled *First Thoughts*. She supported him in his musical career, whereas his father wanted him to become a banker. Johann took secret violin lessons, and when his father deserted the family to live with his mistress, he became the family's sole support.

Johan Strauss II conducting his band.

Young Johann made his concert debut, age 18, at the smart Dommayer's Casino, playing the violin and conducting. He was an immediate success and his own *Sinngedichte Walzer* ("Epigram Waltzes"), Opus 1, were encored five times. After his father's death in 1849, Johann II merged their two orchestras and was acclaimed the new "Waltz King," delighting audiences at home and abroad. Following the success of Offenbach's operettas, Strauss decided to compose for the stage, writing his masterpiece *Die Fledermaus* in 1874. He continued to write operettas and provide his

inimitable waltzes for Viennese balls (*left*). Strauss died peacefully in his sleep in 1899 and was given the ultimate honor of being buried beside such musical giants as Beethoven, Schubert and Brahms.

KEY NOTES

In 1872, Strauss II accepted an invitation to come to Boston to participate in the "International Peace Jubilee." More than 30,000 musicians and singers assembled for this event.

EDVARD GRIEG *1843–1907*

Wedding Day at Troldhaugen

OPUS 65

Grieg wrote this fanciful piece for his wife Nina in 1892, for their 25th wedding anniversary, which was celebrated at their mountain home, Troldhaugen. Grieg was by this time a famous national figure in Norway and the couple received gifts from all over the country, including a Steinway grand piano. In the evening, Grieg sat down at the new piano and played this tribute to his marriage. The music begins as a jaunty march, followed by a gentle swaying section. The march returns, resuming the jovial mood, and the piece proceeds merrily to its conclusion.

LYRICAL EXPRESSIONS

Wedding Day at Troldhaugen is one of Grieg's *Lyric Pieces*, which he wrote to express his most personal thoughts.

KEY NOTES

Nina and Edvard were so attached to their mountain home at Troldhaugen that they arranged to remain close to it after their deaths. Their ashes are sealed in a cliff overlooking the house.

SERGEI PROKOFIEV *1891–1953*

Symphony No.1 in D Major

"CLASSICAL," OPUS 25: FINALE

Explaining the inspiration behind his symphony, Prokofiev said, "Had Haydn lived to our day he would have retained his own style while accepting something of the new... This was the kind of symphony I wanted to write." In this, the last movement, he was clearly in high spirits, rounding off a work that he was aware could become a classic. The mood is joyful and playful, as breathless strings and woodwinds race each other, tumbling over in the carefree melody, like a gaggle of ragamuffins at play. While adopting the Classical style, the music remains remarkably modern and, above all, joyous.

TROUBLED TIMES

Surprisingly, this carefree work was written while Prokofiev's native Russia was in turmoil. The army was suffering terrible losses in the war with Germany, and the Revolution of 1917 was about to result in civil war.

KEY NOTES

Until 1917, Prokofiev composed at the piano. However, having no instrument at hand when he wrote this piece, he composed without one—and often did so later.

FRANZ LEHÁR *1870–1948*

The Merry Widow

O VATERLAND

*I*n Act One of this operetta, a ball is held in Paris at the embassy of a fictional Balkan country, Pontevedro. One of the guests is Hanna Glawari, a rich widow who the ambassador hopes will marry Count Danilo, nephew of the Pontevedrian king. Danilo arrives from the famous restaurant Maxim's, with six "grisettes" (cabaret dancers) in tow. He sings this simple but endearing song, about his tedious life serving the "fatherland" in Paris. Solace comes only at night when, as he buoyantly declares, "Ich gehe zu Maxim" ("I go off to Maxim's"). With delight, he gives the pet names of the girls with him: "Lolo, Dodo, JouJou, Froufrou, Cloclo, Margot," then falls asleep in an alcove, not even realizing he is about to meet his first true love—Hanna.

THE MILLIONAIRE COMPOSER

The most successful composer of operetta in the 20th century, Franz Lehár grew up in Hungary where his father was an army bandleader. Lehár's own musical promise was fostered, and he studied the violin at the Prague Conservatory from the age of 12. A story tells how he showed Dvořák some sonatas he had written, at which the great composer told him to hang up his fiddle and concentrate on writing.

At first Lehár followed his father as military bandmaster, a post which took him to Vienna in 1899. Lehár wrote several waltzes and operettas before his dazzling hit of 1905, *The Merry Widow*. This made his name internationally and triggered a brisk sideline in "Merry Widow" bonnets, corsets and cocktails. More operettas followed, including *The Count of Luxembourg*, and *Land of Smiles* and *Giuditta*. These operettas were written especially for the great tenor Richard Tauber, who ensured a wide audience with his powerful voice and debonair personality. Lehár died in Switzerland in 1948, leaving a musical legacy that included 38 operettas and several film scores.

HIGH SOCIETY

The world-famous Maxim's (*below*) was founded in 1893, when a waiter, Maxime Gaillard, decided to open his own bar and restaurant. In 1900, the World Exhibition brought a huge, wealthy clientele to Paris, which set Maxim's on an international footing. It became a fashionable venue, known for its exquisite food and luxurious decor. Today part of a worldwide chain, the original restaurant on the Rue Royale still evokes visions of a long bygone age.

KEY NOTES

In its first year, The Merry Widow was performed more than 5,000 times in the U.S., and also had five simultaneous productions in five languages in Buenos Aires. As a result, Lehár was a millionaire at age 35.

ANTONIN DVOŘÁK *1841–1904*

Carnival Overture

OPUS 92

Beginning with a joyous outburst, Dvořák's overture includes enough changes of pace and tone to serve a whole symphony. One moment the music is crashing along with reckless abandon, like a party in full swing, and next it glides gracefully through a gentler section as if the revellers were catching their breath. When Dvořák wrote the *Carnival Overture* in 1891, he was about to depart for the U.S. Given the celebratory mood of the piece, it would seem Dvořák gave himself a truly rousing send-off.

THREE IN ONE

Carnival Overture is one of three concert overtures written together and intended for performance as a group. Originally called *Nature, Life* and *Love*, in 1894 they were renamed *In Nature's Realm, Carnival* and *Othello* for publication as individual works.

CARNIVAL TIME

Originally linked with religious festivals, the word "carnival" has its roots in the medieval Italian "carne vale," meaning farewell to meat. This refers to the fasting period of Lent, when Christians traditionally abstain from meat, eggs and milk. Lent begins on Ash Wednesday, approximately six weeks before Easter, and in Catholic countries the week before is often devoted to feasting and merrymaking, in anticipation of the lean times ahead. This is the origin of the famous New Orleans carnival known as "Mardi Gras," French for "Fat Tuesday." The German and Austrian festival of "Fasching" is also a pre-Lent celebration, as is the world-renowned Rio carnival in Brazil. In more restrained Britain, a celebration takes place on Shrove Tuesday, the day before Ash Wednesday, when all the milk and eggs are used up, traditionally in the form of pancakes.

The Rio carnival, celebrated with typical Brazilian exuberance.

FAREWELL TOUR

In 1892, before embarking for the U.S., Dvořák travelled around Europe on a five–month farewell tour. He was accompanied by the cellist Hanuš Wihan (*standing on right*) and violinist Ferdinand Lachner (*seated*). With Dvořák (*middle*) at the piano, the trio was nicknamed the "Dumky Trio," after the composer's work of the same name.

KEY NOTES

Carnival Overture *was dedicated by Dvořák to the University of Prague, in gratitude for the Doctorate of Philosophy that it had conferred on him in 1890.*

Credits & Acknowledgments

PICTURE CREDITS

Cover /Title and Contents Pages/ IBC:
Eric Kamp/ INDEX STOCK, AKG London: 3(tl),
9(bl); Bridgeman Art Library, London/Museum
of London (Samuel Wale:Vauxhall Gardens) 4(b),
Historisches Museum Der Stadt, Vienna (Charles
Wilda: Strauss and Lanner - "The Ball") 5, Gavin
Graham Gallery, London (Georges Fraipont:
Place de la Concorde, Paris) 7(bl), Bibliothèque
de l'Arsenal, Paris (Breviary of René II of
Lorraine) 13(tl), Manchester City Art Galleries
(James Jacques Tissot: Hush! The Concert) 15,
Christie's Images (Alois Schonn: A Masked Ball
in a Theatre) 18, Historisches Museum Der Stadt,
Vienna (Franz Kollarz (after): Sophien-Bad-Saal,
a Court Ball in the Hoffburg Palace) 19(b),
Historisches Museum Der Stadt, Vienna

(Theodore Zasche: The Johann Strauss Orchestra
at a Court) 19(t), Nationalmuseum, Stockholm
(August Malstrom: Children Playing) 21; Pierre
Cardin: 23(r); Corbis-Bettmann/UPI: 13(tr);
Mary Evans Picture Library: 4(t), 7(tl & br),
9(tr), 10(tr & b), 13(bl), 17(bl), 24; Explorer:12;
Fine Art Photographic Library: (John Austen
Fitzgerald: The Enchanted Forest) 11, Mensing
Gallery, Hamm-Rhynen, Germany (A Scharer:
The Wedding) 20; Getty Images: 3(r), 25(t);
Images: 6; Lebrecht Collection: 10(tl), 17(r), 22,
23(l), 25(b); Performing Arts Library/Clive Barda
8, Ron Scherl 16, 17(tl); The Stock Market: 2;
Veuve Clicquot (UK) Ltd: 3(bl); Reg Wilson: 14

All illustrations and symbols: John See